Excerpts from …

The Dream Journals

J. C. Mellor

 A catalogue record for this book is available from the National Library of Australia

Copyright © 2025 J.C. Mellor
All rights reserved.
ISBN-13: 978-1-923174-54-2

Linellen Press
265 Boomerang Road
Oldbury, Western Australia
www.linellenpress.com.au

Dedication

To My Mother
(A promise well kept!)

Contents

Dedication iii
Contents v
A Bitter Lesson 1
A Canvas of Memories 2
A Closet of Misunderstandings 3
A Day Like This 4
A Day of Little Smiles 6
A Dream 8
A Memory of You 9
A Million Moments 10
A Moment In Time 11
A Mother's Day Wish 12
A Place To Live 13
A Season Long Gone 15
A Thin Life 16
A Thousand Wishes 17
About Priority 18
Alive on Rooftops 19
All Those Splendid Flowers 20
All Together 21
Alone With Me 22
As I Lie Awake 23
As the Crow Flies 24

At One with the Trees	25
Autumn	26
Beautiful Day	27
Before the Sun Goes Down	28
Bouncing Off Walls	29
Caterpillars, Screaming	30
Changes	32
Cold Winter Days	33
Creatures of the Day	35
Evening Comes	36
Flight	37
Flimsy Whimsy	38
For the Love	39
Friendship	41
From Nature's Vine	42
Funny Little Ways	43
Gardening Fun	44
Good Friends	45
Good News	46
Goodnight, Shakespeare	47
Green Eyed	48
Happiness is Free	49
Hey, Mate	50

Hope	51
How Do I Know?	52
I Love Thunder Storms	53
In Eternal Rest	55
In the Forest of the Night	57
In the Morning of Today	58
In the Splendid Place of Night	59
In Those Cold Places	60
Inside, Looking Out	61
Just Wishful Thinking	62
Little White Lies	64
Living in Dreams	65
Looking After Myself	67
Midnight Sun	69
Mothers' Purpose	70
My Autumn Leaf Friends	71
My Daughter	72
My Happy Day	73
My Old Friend	75
Nature's Story	76
No Argument	77
Of My Story	79
Oh, Man of Passion	80

Old Suburban Streets	81
On These Days	84
Purpose	85
Sadness is Heavy	86
Sink Before You Swim!	87
Slowly, Slowly	89
Stairway to the Moon	90
Sue	92
Summer Rain	94
That Clever Woman	95
That Old Magpie	96
That Sweet Escape	97
That Touch	98
The Deck	99
The End	100
The Glory of a Tree	101
The Moon and I	102
The Next Hundred Years	104
The Power of Imagination	106
The Red Rose	107
The Sea of Lost Humanity	108
The Sloth	110
The Solitary Storm	111

The Task-Master 112

The Thief of Time 113

The Troubled Dream 114

The Warmth of an Autumn Day 115

The Watchers 117

The Willow Tree 118

Through the Crack 120

To Count The Lucky Starlit Sky 121

Today's Wonders 122

Traveller of Thoughts 123

To Turn on a Dime 124

Until Mornings' Light 125

Walking With String 126

Warm Summer's Night 128

Warm Winter's Day 129

Where the Passion Lives 130

Without Imagination 131

You Are 132

About the Author 134

A Bitter Lesson

When it comes to reason, there is little gain,
But much to learn, though nothing to purchase,
Yet much to earn when life turns round and round
Again, leaving you spinning and writhing in pain.

For there is ever a season in which to sleep,
But never to rest and always to weep,
Yet much to ponder and more to regret
And the rest of the lesson, my friend, will keep!

A Canvas of Memories

Beyond the gentle rise and fall of the landscape
the trees blossom in reds and greens, purples and blues.
The hues of a summer's day
Leave out all the shades of grey, lifting the curious eye
to the rainbow brilliance of the gardens in the meadows.

Oasis of trees stands gossiping, protecting the newborn,
Keeping furtive watch over the fruit
of their diminishing existence,
And, when the rains come,
they dance in the wind, waving at the sky,
Greeting the clouds as they thunder on by.

This, after all, is what they Live for.
My eyes take in this splendour
and my heart fills with gratitude,
For, in such a short time, the dark will come
and I will be left with a blank canvas,
painted only with my lingering memories.

A Closet of Misunderstandings

Sadness wears many hats,
Parading about in the latest fashions,
a part of the 'in' crowd, disguised,
anonymous - Invisible.

Loneliness wears a magic cloak,
Hiding in shadows from prying eyes
And wagging tongues and censure
or judgements - unbidden.

Disappointment wears several masks,
dressed to hide from accusing eyes
or arrogant stares, or disapproving
glances - Badly hidden.

Grief hides in hat-boxes,
or in the places in which masks
are stored, afraid of exposure,
Where sorrow is forbidden.

Love is blatant – parading itself
In full view, too often mistaken
by a less truer heart, or, like a show
pony - real love is badly ridden.

A Day Like This

(In memory of the Boxing Day Tsunami)

I never knew a day like this,
Balmy skies and turquoise oceans,
Gentle breezes blowing
Friendly laughter in the air
Sumptuous feasts and goodwill flowing.

I never knew a day like this,
People joking, families playing,
Beer and goodwill flowing,
A rumble felt way underneath
But we partied on, not knowing.

I never knew a day like this,
People shouting, standing, staring,
Partying still, not knowing,
Ignoring calls to run, run, run,
As the wind began its awful blowing.

I never knew a day like this,
Screams of terror, people drowning,
The wind was still a-blowing,
Plucked like feathers, cars and people
In the boiling waters, seas a-growing.

I never knew a day like this,
As in a dream I ran in terror,
To escape the sea a-growing,
Fighting to survive the death
That towards came swiftly flowing.

I never knew a day like this,
Now, all alone, my loved ones missing
In the sea fast flowing,
Lost, or drowned, the cries of wounded
And those gone to God, all-knowing.

A Day of Little Smiles

The bright blue sky looked cheerful
So I took a little walk;
I met some people on the way,
And some folk stopped to talk.

A woman with a little dog
said "How are you today?"
I answered, "I am very well!"
Then we went on our way.

A man who wore a funny hat
was sitting on a bench
Reading last week's paper,
while enjoying his lunch.

Some children with their mother
chased a bright red ball.
They had strayed a bit too far
until their mother's call.

The lady with the little dog
came by me once again,
And, to the dog with a little smile
said "It's time for home now, Ben!"

The man had finished lunch, it seemed,
And read the paper through.
He gave me a little smile,
Tipped his hat with a 'how'd you do!'

A pretty little waitress
Showed patrons to their seat
At tables on the sidewalk,
Ordering food to eat.

Seagulls squawked so loudly,
And fought over scraps of food.
I drank the scene in happily
Enjoying the festive mood.

I looked across the Estuary
At a family at play
And lovers soaking in the sunshine
As on the grass they lay.

I loved that happy feeling
As the warmth soaked through my skin.
Then I turned and made my way back home
Wearing a happy grin!

A Dream

A dream
is a complex jigsaw puzzle
of events and memories,
caught up and expelled
from the psyche during repose
when the mind relaxes and the day
And all its taxes are at a close.

A Memory of You

Long hours passing, panting, breathing,
Waiting for that life anew,
I am here, I am there, drifting, hoping
For one glimpse of you.

Long hours stretching, dreaming, crying,
Wishing pain would go away,
And then, the moment, hopeful, wistful,
Heading to the close of day.

More long hours, drifting, struggling,
Then that moment, dreams come true
When I hear that tiny person –
My first loving touch of you.

I felt empty, over-flowing
With the love that mothers knew
Since the first amazing moment,
The conception of the one that's you.

A Million Moments

Life is built on a million moments,
a zillion smiles, and a trillion tears.
Moments are the best foundation
To help us grow throughout the years.

Moments are Life's truest mortar
That keeps us together as we grow,
With each new event we build our future,
And cement the past with all we know.

Life will thrive as each moment happens,
As we choose our course as days go by,
And then, when time is long behind us –
Our moments will last long after we die.

A Moment In Time

Time.
A moment.
Clock ticking.
Hands moving.
Hands resting.

Birth.
A miracle.
Reproducing.
Propagating.
Being.

Joy.
Caring.
Sharing.
Reaching.
Loving.

Death.
Memories.
Loved ones.
Kindnesses.
Ending.

A Mother's Day Wish

I have no heart for disappointment
On this, our National Mother's Day –
Nor dare I hope for some fulfilment
Thinking things might come my way.

I am filled with such a longing
That my dreams, today, come true –
All I need is one small message –
A heartfelt 'hello' straight from you!

A Place To Live

I want to live in a good place
That wants me to live in it –
A place that understands my story
Long before I begin it.

I want to live in a time
That's filled with the love of friends –
A time that knows its boundaries,
Where it starts and where it ends.

I want to feel at home
No matter where I stay –
As long as we all can share
The privilege of going grey.

I want to laugh and sing
From July until June –
And nobody minds at all
If my song is out of tune.

I want to be safe and warm
Through all of Nature's seasons –
To give and take of love and life
Without searching for reasons.

And when my final day is done
I'll pass on all my treasure
And pray that those who follow on
will think of me with pleasure!

A Season Long Gone

I long for the day when my body is kind,
And the thought of illness is gone from my mind,
And the aches and the pains are just old memories
Of times before, when I had my young knees.

I pray that my body will very soon heal,
And the feeling of health is again very real,
And my joints are all limber without any ache
As I spring from my bed the moment I wake.

I hope that the time will come really quick
When I wake in the morning without feeling sick,
And the heat of the day is a season long gone,
And the sweet sound of rain on the roof lingers on.

When was the last time that I felt fit and well
Instead of my stomach burning like Hell,
Or my muscles all hurting as I move each part
And the fear of something going wrong with my heart?

As each morning brings yet another new ache
I try to keep faithful each promise I make
To keep off the couch and exercise more
So my body will move as it once moved before!

A Thin Life

I have lived a life of loneliness
In this skin, of this time,
Where misunderstandings grow
And I am thin, far too thin.

I have often dreamed of nothingness,
In this skin, far too thin,
There is little here I have to show
In this time, of this skin.

I wander in the wilderness,
In this skin, old and thin,
With heavy heart of needs and woe,
In this life, far too thin.

For nothing is what we come with
In this life but this skin,
And take it when we choose to go,
from this skin, a life too thin, too thin.

A Thousand Wishes

A child can only dream of fairies
After the first fairytale she's heard;
She can only understand love
If she's felt it – deed and word.

A child can make a thousand wishes,
Count her lucky if one comes true;
But, love and wishes are like dreams
The best is but far and few.

I have dreamed a thousand wishes,
And wished for a love – sweet and kind,
But, like those dreams that soon vanish
Along with hope – out of sight and mind.

I have lived a life of interest
Where many things have come and gone,
But, my wish for love is fading –
Yet the dream of it goes on and on … and on.

About Priority

I travel through the mists of time
Searching for a pleasing rhyme
With which to keep me company
On this, my Life's journey.

I walk across the fields of fire,
Through the nettles and the mire,
The lessons of this time to learn –
And for the love I yearn.

If I should stumble on the way
I know that dearly I shall pay,
Unless the mistakes I endure
Teach me about priority.

Alive on Rooftops

Oh, give me ravings and midnight cravings,
And endless walks on rooftops far above
The cacophony of city streets.
Let me wander over the hidden places,
Those voids and spaces unseen, sky-clean,
Where vistas of chimneys and skeleton aerials
seem neat.

I yearn for the height and the awful sight
Of concrete gardens filled with clouds.
It is all I need to feel complete.
Yet, once I'm there after climbing every agonising
Stair, I shed my filthy city skin, sucking clean air in,
Crowing as the city – dark and grimy, accepts at last
- defeat!

All Those Splendid Flowers

From my verandah, I sit and contemplate the day,
Watching the breeze toss the leaves far and away,
And smile as the birds, busy with work and play
Make the most of the daylight hours.

I know it won't last, for each season, in its own time,
Must hand over to the next, keeping alive the rhyme
Of Nature's poetry, each verse, in its purity, sublime
After each of Autumn's showers.

I'm melancholy, caught in each moment as it fades
As the sun shrugs into its evening bed and wades
Into the horizon, night upon night, for so many decades,
As we, too, fade like all those splendid flowers.

All Together

Let me hold the moment as the sun pulls away,
And clouds paint the sky with many coats of grey,
and the birds are too busy going about their day
as aloneness surrounds me, and I sigh.

The world goes on as the dusk follows dawn,
And I long for the dreaming to get me through 'til morn,
For I feel the echoes from the time since I was born
But my eyes, like my old skin, feel so dry.

I hurt for those whose dear mem'ries have gone
Into the void where today lives on and on and on,
And I give such heartfelt thanks that I am not alone,
that we'll all be together, by and by.

Alone With Me

I am alone –
I need not fear it –
I don't have to bear it –
I can wear it
Or give myself over to tears.

But, I will not give to it
My energy -
Or my loyalty –
Or my vitality –
Or my sanity –

Aloneness cannot steal
All those parts that
Make me real -
For they are all part of me –
They are what make me – me!

As I Lie Awake

I find reprieve in the spoken word,
From that awful and insidious fear
Born of being too much alone –
Though family lives so very near.

I find solace in the talking books,
So soothing through the darker hours
As I lie awake 'til the early dawn,
Comforted by technology's powers.

As the Crow Flies

It is not always the shortest route
As the crow flies –
Nor is it a shortcut to our destiny
In a straight line.

I cannot see above the stately trees,
Or know where my fate lies –
if it was pre-ordained for us all
even by the Divine.

I would marvel at the breath-taking view
From the clear, blue skies
If I saw what the crows can see
Over Tuart and Pine.

I am bound to meander over land,
Even though Man tries
To conquer the sky like Crows,
But in a crooked line!

At One with the Trees

I fasten myself to a tree
And hold tight to its trunk.
It steadies me;
Gives me a sense of safety.

I feel its heartbeat,
I hear its blood flowing.
It gives me what I need -
Warmth and purpose.

I am filled with such joy
As I hold it tight –
As its spirit holds me,
And gives me strength.

I revel in its community
And feel at one with the tree
As if I, too, belong
To its majestic family.

Let me stay, I say,
Until I can stand alone,
And the tree sighs
when finally, I walk away.

Autumn

Oh, autumn, how sublime you are,
Dressed in your finery of olive green and russet red,
Skipping about the earth
Sprinkling drying leaves on my head.

From summer, you cool us, gently and slowly,
As you stand before your easel and draw
Tomorrow's vibrant scene,
then dress it in gold and green, autumn's colour.

Beautiful Day

It's a beautiful day for being at home,
for keeping my own company.
It's a wonderful day for doing those chores
that keep on eluding me.

I smile at the sky, so blue, fresh and clear,
and it smiles at me in the same way.
I could want for no other perfect reward
than to be home on this beautiful day!

Before the Sun Goes Down

I love you from a distance,
Through the clouds, Across the sea.
I love you to the moon and back,
You're never far from me.

I love you till the cows come home,
From dusk 'til break of day.
No matter all the miles between,
You're never far away.

I love you when you take my hand,
Or hug me with your heart.
You're just a short phone call from me,
That's not so far apart!

But if we fight, the distance grows,
And my body seems to frown,
So we can sleep we'd best make up
Before the sun goes down!

Bouncing Off Walls

Long years have passed and I have gleaned
A wealth of learning, yearning to be good,
As most people should. Yet, somehow,
Time has come and gone too fast, and I,
In my senescence, know that there is still
so much to learn.

I learned that, for all I think, and all I am,
I am less than perfect, but, I understand
That perfection is, in itself, an imperfect
State, and, as my precious destiny calls,
I must wait here, spending time
bouncing off walls!

Caterpillars, Screaming

(For Ron)

In the last breath of time, when all things grow dim,
And the dust begins to settle on old memories –
I think of him.

I see the photos, and somehow, now they make more
sense, for there is no pretense, and I finally understand
When I think of him.

I recall that unforgettable day when he took my hand and
smiled and turned to me and said, "Listen! Am I
dreaming?" and I think of him.

"Or can you, too, hear the sound of caterpillars
screaming?" He was so ill then, as, like the photos,
they remind me of him.

The caterpillars marched onwards despite the cars
that crushed over that hot, dirty line thinking all was fine,
just like him.

He knew the pain of each one crawling in the dust
beneath the April sun, going on with trust –
just like him.

His sweet goodbye will always bring a tear to my eye,
And when I revisit that precious snapshot in time -
It will remind me of him.

He is gone now, and I can smile when I see those photos of caterpillars purposely marching forward, much as he did to the end – and – I will always think of him.

Changes

Isn't it strange how a body can change,
How fears may come and then go?
Isn't it weird how the things that we feared -
When faced are all act and no show?

And, isn't it bad when we should feel sad -
But the heart feels nothing at all?
But, there's none to compare with a soul without care -
for a child who's known no love at all!

Isn't it strange how a body can change,
How the years go by in a flash.
Isn't it weird how the things that I feared
Are all spent, and I don't mean like cash!

Isn't it sad that I should feel bad
When my life is fading to grey?
But there's none to compare to
a life one can't share,
Or a heart left to just waste away!

Cold Winter Days

I love the city on cold winter days -
the sound of tyres squishing on
black ribbon roads like tearing paper -
busy feet in drowning, wet leather -
hats over frizzled hair - long black coats
on tall, elegant men, slapping along in bi-ped
motion - and faces, pink and fresh,
sporting bespoiled make-up under feeble
umbrellas, trying in vain to escape
from newly shed winter's tears.

I love the smell of oil and petrol fumes,
Old autumn dust, settled without permission,
Now removed from crusty leaves on executive
streets - for once devoid of city grime;
the footpaths crazy and slick and worn,
weathered and washed free of pieces
of soggy debris and truant papers stuck
fast to its skin while city-slickers
hide in pretence of shopping -
waiting for the deluge to cease.

I love the city's music – a cacophony
of drum-beat rain and rubbish-bin cymbals –
discordant honking horns and mobile phones –
garbled chatter and choruses of muted laughter –
a melody of city life which marches to the beat
of its own drum, and, how I love the moment
when showers are done - crowds grow thin -
cars crawl towards welcome and much warmer
homes, and work halts until tomorrow
when the new day comes.

Then, I love the washed, haunting quiet
As the last damp, sensible shoes echo
in the aftermath of that bustling life.
It is not for everyone - but, as I watch
commuters forging into the darkening day,
bracing against the wind as they hurry
homewards sipping takeaway lattes,
and stepping into the cold embrace
of sliding doors - I smile at the city
on those cold, winter days!

Creatures of the Day

Do faeries really hide from sight
From humans who come out at night
While others use the light of day
To avoid dark things of prey?

In the forests of the day
All magic beings hideaway
And, only those with faerie sight
Can see the creatures of the night!

Evening Comes

Evening comes,
And the soft blush of the summer sun
Washes the skies with delicate lavender hues
which linger on the mind's eye
till the azure cloak of night falls.

The cry of the gull interrupts the song
And playful dogs bark as the dark descends,
Far too eager to replace the glorious scene
With man-made illumination, hiding
The splendour of Nature's creation.

The lull deepens and draws me in,
And even in the sultry air, I feel my cares
And woes depart, and the joy of evening
Lingers in my tattered, worn-out heart
Until morning comes again!

Flight

If I could escape this world
and remove myself from
this sorry sight,
I would take to the wing
until peace falls back
and things become right,
then, like the birds on high,
I, too, would take flight.

I would soar among clouds
on high and fall upon
the rain's own head
if I could fly, but, till then,
I will have to be content
with today's mayhem
filled with avarice and spite,
for wings don't grow overnight!

Here, in this upset world,
bad things have become right,
but I prefer simpler things,
and would, with little might,
escape until the anger goes
and is replaced by peace;
then, like the dove, we all
  could take flight!

Flimsy Whimsy

There's a flimsy, whimsy 'whatabout'
whinging round my 'why's;
A clumsy, bumsy 'just because'
Is singing round my sighs.

And with every natter, chatter,
Clattering through my head,
My 'pitter-patter' keeps me going
Not wishing I was dead.

A nagging, ragging, scolding pointer
Pokes a painful hole
Into my once-was-wider pride
and left a simpering soul

A pleading, needing 'cannot'
Chokes and pokes the 'do's'
And I'm slipping, sliding, drowning
In a sea of 'I love you's.'

For the Love

I was given a world of colour and people,
Of value and reward - a good world.
I was given a family, fractured and disjointed,
Disfunctional, yet functioning.
I was endowed with abilities,
unrecognised, misunderstood,
but used and enjoyed.
I was granted a love of music and poetry,
Able to pour out my heart in song.
I was taught values without example,
Left to make decisions about those values.
I was given space and freedom to learn,
Yet the learning was fractured and hard.
I was dealt with both fairly and firmly,
Not always understanding, or understood.
I was given a deep acknowledgement
Of the mysteries and complexities of life.
I was exposed to bad things, and good things,
And left to choose my own path.
I took the right path – for me – yet got lost
Along the way when unsupported.
I was many things, yet I am no more than
Myself for all life's sorrows and joys.
I have yet to explore the years to come,

And, no matter how many, I will endure.
I was given this life, and have become wiser
For it all,
yet I know not who to thank for it!
Perhaps, that is the next part of my journey,
And I will smile through it and be grateful
For the love.

Friendship

Cheery smiles, happy chatter -
Walks along the lane -
Whistling kettles and fine bone china
Next day, start again.

Movies, groups, meetings, fun
Helps the day go by,
But friendship's what it's all about -
We need it, you and I!

From Nature's Vine

I've travelled far along the road –
Following the way, unknown
Without a visible guiding hand,
Without a path that's shown.

Though many a slip passed underfoot,
And many a trip to trap me –
I managed to stay one step ahead
Of obstacles laid before me.

For fifty years I shared the load;
Two-thirds of my life left behind
With one-third of autonomy,
And the rest – yet left to find.

I filled my cup and took a sip –
And tasted Life's bitter-sweet wine,
But who really wants to drink alone
The nectar from Nature's vine?

Funny Little Ways

My funny little ways may be hard to abide,
But most of my friends take me in their stride,
And hardly worry that I can't see
For I'm rarely found without company.

Of course, we can't please every living soul,
So, having a few good friends is my goal,
And I am surrounded by kind, loving folk
Who can share with me some gossip or a joke.

Friends like these are treasures to know
And keep the fire in my heart a-glow
As we spend our time passing the days
Sharing each other's funny little ways.

Gardening Fun

Smell the earth, fresh and sweet,
Soft and warm beneath the feet.
Plant the seeds; watch them grow,
And soon, small shoots begin to show!

As the seedlings start to thrive
Remember, care keeps them alive.
Water them well; give them care
And soon, you'll have vegetables to share!

Good Friends

To all the friends I've known
And the kindnesses you've shown –
I wish to send a 'thank you'
From the heart

For you've filled my life with sunshine
With your caring, thoughtful ways –
And even through Life's winter –
You have warmed those colder days.

So, thank you for your kindnesses,
For those special times we've shared –
Those memories will stay with me
Even when we are apart!

Good News

(For my daughter)

I just heard the news today,
It seems a new life's on its way!
In months ahead we'll watch it grow.
This is the best time that you'll know!

No better love is found on Earth
Than what you'll share at your child's birth.
We wish for you the very best,
For parenthood is quite a test!

But, also, that you'll find great joy
Forever, with your girl or boy.
When you watch your child at play
Remember how you felt today.

Goodnight, Shakespeare

I'd say 'goodnight' in several ways
If I lived in old Shakespeare's days,
But it would thus end all the same,
Even if spoke by a less-known name!

I'd wish you all a fond adieu
And pray you'd sleep the whole night through
In sweet surrender to the night,
As would Shakespeare, wrong or right!

I think he'd find some clever phrase
To give the moon celestial praise,
And then, to bed, and thus – to sleep –
And pledge his heart for Love to keep!

Green Eyed

He loves to find you waiting
At night when he comes home.
He talks to you, he smiles at you;
He frets when you are gone.

He worries if you sleep too much,
Or you maybe miss a meal.
He cuddles you and hugs you:
His love for you is real.

He shares his inner feelings
With you when you're alone.
He shows you unconditional love
No matter what you've done!

No wonder I am jealous,
I'd kill for some of that!
But, I am just his girlfriend
And you, his precious cat!

Happiness is Free

There is happiness all around,
Passed from hand to hand
Without question or payment
By neighbours, family and friends.

It is there for all to embrace
And easy to understand
Without a trace of censure,
Or the desire to pretend.

Happiness should be shared,
Not just on demand
Without a price or value,
or a beginning and an end.

Hey, Mate

(In Memory of Morrie 1929-2024)

Hey, mate – I'm thinking of you –
You are often on my mind
As I think of our dear friendship –
The very best of friends you'll find.

Hey, friend – You're in my thoughts –
As I think back to earlier days
When we both wrote and shared our words,
Both writing in our separate ways.

Hey, pal – I'm glad to know you –
Friends like you are hard to find,
So, I had to take the time to tell you –
That you're always on my mind!

Hey, mate – I'm smiling at you –
As I recall the helping hand
You offer all your friends who love you,
As friends go – mate – you are grand!

Hope

What better way to cope
When one is prone to mope
About the house all day
In search of occupation?

I tend to choose something light
To ease away the frustration
Of being alone so long,
And set my sights on Hope!

How Do I Know?

How do I know what tomorrow may bring,
If the sun will rise, if the birds will sing?
How can I say what will come my way
So, I'll embrace the day, regardless!

How will I know if I'll laugh and smile
With my friends as we sit and chat for awhile?
How can I guess if I'll have a good day
If I choose to be moody and restless?

I cannot know what Fate has in store,
Or what Destiny chooses to lay at my door,
Unless I take a chance and go out to play
And pass the new day filled with kindness!

I Love Thunder Storms

I have little to do here
Except lie and wile away the hours
Watching the changing skies,
And the clouds darkening with threatening
showers as the setting sun sinks gently,
slipping into its crimson bed
As the thunderclouds
Pull the covers over its head.

Then, watching the night creep in,
I wait, silently holding my breath
As the first distant peels of thunder
Announce its rage;
the lightning flashes angrily
across my bed;
yet I am not afraid;
I am excited as I wait for the show.

Even when the door creaks
In response to the wind
Moaning through my window –
most children would feel afraid -
but, not I,
for, lying here under my covers,
I escape like the wind,
And, like the thunder - I roar!

No, this I do not fear,
for this is mild in comparison
to the storm that rages inside,
Which ebbs and flows,
as, like my limbs and hair,
with great propensity - it grows.
But, beside the other things
a lost child fears, this is not one!

Fear does not lie within Nature's beauty,
or the passion of pending storms,
only in my own mind,
and I may fear the creaking door,
The lashing of the howling wind,
or electric flash of lightning -
but be sure –
I do love thunder storms!

In Eternal Rest

Worry not, my friend, my friend,
The best things in life must end,
But memories will always be
A part of our own history.

I did so much in younger days,
Some of which is just a haze,
But, at times, when each arises
It fills my heart with sweet surprises.

Not everything we do or see
Is worthy of such memory,
And so, we savour what is best,
And put to bed the awful rest.

I've stories yet to tell, it seems,
That manifest in my new dreams,
And, like a movie I once saw,
Can leave me craving for some more.

And so, I say, to all who know
How reminiscing lets us glow
As we recount those treasured years,
As joy converts to managed fears.

So, worry not, my friend, my friend,
The best things in life might end,
But we hold on to what seems best
To keep us warm in eternal rest.

In the Forest of the Night

Everything is out of sight
In the Forest of the Night
Where Earth is marked by dappled light
And beauty lives on pure and bright.

Everything is lost, away
From the garish light of day
And Nature thrives, come what may
And nothing, then, is tossed away.

Trees grow tall despite all men,
All cut down but grown again,
And one day we'll remember when
Trees grew tall, despite all men.

Everything is pure and bright
Where Earth is marked by dappled light,
And beauty lives on out of sight
In the Forest of the Night.

In the Morning of Today

I am in the morning of Today,
As far away from Yesterday
As Time allows; my choice -
To fill the hours on my demand,
As I understand the movement
Of Time and all its tomorrows.

I am prepared for skies of grey
No matter how bright the sun,
For Today has begun in sunshine,
But it's a long road till night,
And it's my right to ponder the hours
or waste them in past sorrows.

In the Splendid Place of Night

In the splendid place of night
One may drift into the void
Where fantasy and fact divide,
And sometimes, vanish out of sight.

In this realm of fractured dreams
One might live a life so strange
That playrights dare not use their craft
To copy down the fiercest scenes.

One is carried from Night's play
Out of myth's or magic's lair,
And wakes with apprehension's dread
Back in the cold, dull light of Day.

In Those Cold Places

There's an emptiness inside
Where my demons like to hide,
And fears and phobias grow
With little censure;

Where all the pain and tears
Are gathered through the years,
Keeping down Life's beauty
and adventure.

As I pass through those dark days
That should be all ablaze,
Filled with joi d'vivre
And with laughter –

I will strive to fill the spaces
And insert in those cold places
All the love I gather now
And ever after!

Inside, Looking Out

So much has passed beneath the bridge
Borne on my own life's tide;
Much has come and more has gone
To feed ego and pride.
I cannot claim to know much more
Than I'm supposed to know,
And I've been tossed on stormy seas,
Blown where ill winds must blow.

Achievements, I can boast of few,
And of worldly goods, abound,
And I could pave the Moon's own road,
With the sorrows I have found.
Though I could brag about my life,
And from mountain tops could shout
That I have spent much wiser years
On the inside, looking out.

I never was a sparkly child,
But have personality of my own;
I've had three lovely children,
And the affection they have shown
Has nourished me through many droughts
When affection was quite thin,
and often found myself quite stuck
On the inside, looking in.

Just Wishful Thinking

The news was good, I heard him say
The weather would be fine today
And everywhere was harmony.
Animals flourished by the score.
But, it was only wishful thinking.

Happiness grew everywhere.
No pollution spoiled the air,
And the ozone was what it should be.
But, it was only wishful thinking.

No sickness could be found on Earth,
Nor sadness, only joy and mirth.
Prosperity ruled the whole world round.
But, it was only wishful thinking.

My love and I lived happily.
We gazed back at our family tree
Our ancestors would be truly proud
But, it was only wishful thinking.

Our young folk all were good as gold
And never a problem could be told
Of murder, theft or rape, it's true.
But, it was only wishful thinking.

I woke up from this curious dream.
And swallowed down an anguished scream.
Was the happiness I'd known
All just wishful thinking?

Little White Lies

Do not preach to me of friendship
Whilst my enemies you feed.
Do not preach to me of hardship
As you shun all those in need.

Do not sing to me of virtues
As you plot to lie and steal;
Do not sing to me your lovesong
When your intentions are not real.

Do not hand to me a flower
Stolen from a neighbour's yard,
And woo me with a stolen kiss
As if it was won so hard.

Give me just one simple treasure,
On which no price can e'er be set
And I will fill your life with pleasure
And with joy, the best prize yet!

For anyone can tell a story
Filled with lies or pure deceit;
But I'll not boast of a shallow glory
As truth will make true love complete!

Living in Dreams

When dreams abound with hidden treasure
Or tease me with forbidden pleasure
Untouchable though they may seem
I long for just one perfect dream

To sleep, to sleep, I cannot wait
To slip into unconscious state
And leave behind the pain I feel,
Escaping to a world more real.

In dreams I find myself at home
And would, with grace, forever roam
Through the mist where no regret
Can last, as at dawn, I forget.

To dream, to dream, oh, to escape
These tedious days of dubious shape
All melting into one long week,
Till night's repose I dare to seek.

Would I but sleep forever more
If dreams made life worth living for.
But, every conscious breath I take
Prepares me just for dreaming's sake.

Oh, what I'd give, if I could find
One true companion from my mind,
Who, like in dreams, I feel
Could share with me a love that's real!

Looking After Myself

I woke Myself from a dreadful dream,
When I heard Myself softly scream.

It was of demons from Myself's past,
Which made Myself's heart beat so fast!

Myself had woken with such a fright
To find Myself alone that night.

At times like this, Myself felt sad,
Because I was all that Myself had.

The very thought made Myself scared
Because for Myself, no one cared.

So I held Myself tight in my arms,
And soothed Myself of fears and qualms,

And talked to Myself of future dreams,
And shared with Myself, plans and schemes.

I talked till Myself's fears had fled,
Then gently tucked Myself in bed.

Myself felt better, and safer, too!
I was sure Myself would make it through,

For I knew Myself had Me for a friend.
And I'd look after Myself till the end.

Midnight Sun

The snowy peaks loom overhead,
And in the frosty night, I dread the silence.
No words of comfort needed now,
For peace does reign in me, somehow - I sense …

A sweet warmth washes over me,
When, in my mind, your face I see - so clear,
And in the depths of me - I feel
A sweet abandon which is real - my path is set

No loneliness shall hence prevail,
For round the world, I know I'll sail to find my love,
As, from lovers' hands such poems are written
By such as I, who has been smitten by cupid's bow …

And, across the globe to mountains high
I'll fly to you - sweet destiny - with no regrets,
For it is set - our paths shall blend,
As, lovers now, we are good friends till time is done!

No lovers exist such as we;
No heart can fault this ecstacy that we shall know.
So, sleep, my love, till we are one,
With the rising of the midnight sun … we'll be complete

Mothers' Purpose

Time Passes on Wings – They Say!

Silence …
Look past the door
Once more before you close it!
The children are gone!

Ghosts …
Echoes of voices –
Sweet and clear
Invade your peace!

Space …
Loneliness and emptiness -
Too soon the job is done
And chores aren't company!

Thoughts …
Too much thinking –
Looking for purpose –
Listening for footsteps.

Silence …
Look past the door
Tears replace fears –
The mother weeps …
No one knows pain like a mother – they say!

My Autumn Leaf Friends

I have reached that age, it seems,
Where energy is lost in dreams
And other fanciful meanderings
Of a younger self, and childhood things.

I have done so much, it's true,
But still find I have much to do,
But time and age are not friends
Until, at last, our journey ends.

My Daughter

She's the sun in my life, the moon in my sky;
My ocean and rivers that never run dry;
She's my poem, my passion, my lyrics, my song –
The stars in my night, my right and my wrong.

She's my forecast, my weather, my midnight, my noon.
She's my heartbeat, my soul, my cup and my spoon.
She's the wind in my sails helping me get to land –
My friend and advisor, my best helping hand.

She's my coin and my purse – my heart and my soul;
The pride deep within me – my purpose, my goal.
She's the drift of the breeze on a clear autumn day –
The clouds in the sky keeping the sun at bay.

She's my thoughts and my wisdom – My colour and art;
She's the piece of the puzzle – all one and apart.
She's my forest, my mountains, my drought and my water –
So I know God exists for She gave me my daughter!

My Happy Day

I don't like doing the washing,
But I like my clothes to smell clean and fresh,
And when I bring them in, they have the sun
And breeze in them, especially when summer
Has begun.

I like the smell of disinfectant in my rooms
After my cleaner has washed the floors,
And that crisp, sharp smell of bleach,
Touching places elusive dirt might reach
and hide, just for fun.

I like the fragrance of washing powder,
Sweetly scented, on my fresh sheets
When I turn back my bed and prepare
To settle down for the night for a good,
Restful sleep.

I like smooth surfaces after the cloth
Has passed by, removing the grease
And grime of a day's cooking, sometimes
Lazy, sometimes – carefully planned,
Then frozen to keep.

I like floors free of well-trafficked dirt,
Brought in on weary shoes and left
For the vacuum cleaner to discover,
Unable to resist being drawn in
And then, thrown away.

I don't like housework, but I like Home
To be clean and fresh, smelling both
Of me and the busy-ness of my life,
And a little crafty clutter – all part
Of my happy day!

My Old Friend

Where are you, my old friend?
Are you enjoying the garden of your new world,
Where the flowers are living gemstones
That paint such pictures in your mind
Which you include in your dream without end?

I would share those images, if I could,
Or take each one and put them to the canvas
Of my own life, where our thoughts bind –
Even after life, as these words fill the pages.

I am still here, my old friend,
Missing you and your gentle ways and smile,
But I have no regrets, knowing you are here,
Guiding me through to my own life's end!

Nature's Story

As sunlight fades into the horizon,
And the chill of the evening spreads its arms,
I surrender to autumn's embrace,
As it seduces me with its cooler charms.

As the moon settles to watch over us
And illuminates our way in the dark,
I smile up at its round, solemn face,
And in my mind, it leaves its shining mark.

As seasons drift past with every cycle,
I wonder at Life and all its glory,
For nothing here shall be ignored,
As, like us, Nature, too, tells her story!

No Argument

In life, I'd say, my experience
Is vast, some from coincidence,
And other from some eternal plan
That - over a lifetime - it would span!

I'd also claim that what I know
Over the years will surely grow,
But, I'll be no wiser than I'm meant to,
Long after my Life's journey's through.

With arrogance, I could lay claim
To knowledge penned by another's name,
But I don't have the wit to stage
Such a deception, even at this age!

I've travelled far and learned much more
In this long decade and three score –
And so, to claim a brighter brain
Would fill me with sorrow and disdain.

Though some have kindly called me 'smart'
I cannot accept with a humble heart
Any such title, even if I was able
To lay my proof upon the table!

And so – to many faults I'll own
that my wisdom is but home-grown;
As to argue this I would be a fraud
For indeed, I am hopelessly flawed!

Of My Story

I am across all things in a more perfect world,
A font of information and knowledge –
An encyclopaedia of facts and figures,
A genius in mathematics, and never erratic.

I am a legend in my own laptop, wise beyond Time,
Living a life of relative ease and perpetual bliss,
Where nothing goes amiss, and upsets never occur,
Where the sun shines soft and the climate – static.

If such was my world, I would constantly rejoice,
And never fear my voice, or the statements made
By so-called friends that – of my Life's story –
There is much to be told – precise and emphatic!

Oh, Man of Passion

(Tribute to JD)

Oh, man of passion who
Understood mixed delights,
Rejoicing in the beauty of both
Day and night,
Forced to live in hooded darkness
Deprived of a simplistic life
After living in the blessed state
of a paradise known only in fairy tales,
How I wish I knew you well.

Wrenched and torn from the
home you loved,
And, trapped within your living hell
You pondered with a broken heart
And failing will, giving your pain
To those who knew you best,
Recording all the precious times
And those treasures you left behind
In Bougainville.

Old Suburban Streets

I love old suburban streets,
Those narrow bitumen roads and footpaths,
So orderly and easy to navigate -
The spit of sprinklers bursting into life
at daybreak on warm summer mornings
when they come on unannounced -
without warning - as I take my first daily walk.

I love the manicured verges,
trim and neat, and Flame trees
that burst with fire - lining the streets
like old soldiers in smart, red uniforms,
And the autumn-leaf tapestries
That dance at my feet, making nuisance
of themselves on freshly raked lawns.

I love stately old red brick houses
With wide verandahs of polished boards,
And falling-down picket fences,
propped up by geraniums, red and pink;
Children following the bread-cart
and in summer, skipping along
after the ice-man, hoping for a frozen sample.

I love the distant sound of voices,
proper and clear on ABC morning radio,
That marries with the smell of toast burning,
And spoons clinking against cereal bowls,
Mingling with the sweet dew which lingers
On the air of a crisp, spring morning -
Keeping the sounds of breakfast company.

I love old city streets,
Splendid buildings standing proud,
Dressed in architecture crafted by masters,
holding fast against the enemy – Time,
falling at the feet of technology
as I still hear the echo of grumbling trams,
trolley buses and the hiss of steam engines.

I love the poignancy of simpler things
Which old women remember as hard work -
Like the copper, the skiffle board and mangle,
And the lemon-fresh scent of floor polish,
And floors 'we could see our faces in',
All part of the pride of yesteryear
When hard work was really hard!

I miss those days gone by
and the families who went with them;
children too soon grown, surrendering
their toys to tomorrow's ideals,
forgetting a time when memories
were kept in hand-me-down trinket boxes.
And patched up photo albums.

Like me, suburbs have changed and adapted,
surrendered to the destruction of progress
And the love of plastic things that last forever
Unlike us and our keepsakes!
Our unforgettable histories are now left
on dusty shelves, or discarded and overlooked -
like old trees – storytellers of a once simpler life!

Faded are those days -
And that smell of wood stoves, burnt toast
spread with dripping - crackling radio voices,
Cane chairs on wide verandahs around big,
stately houses; the Sunday roast, picnics
and the dear, gentle folk who lived
in those friendly old suburban streets.

On These Days

I'll think on these days
when crisp the wind blows,
and warm the sun shines overhead;
when birds send a cry
to all passers-by,
as soon as the moon is in bed.

I'll think on old times
and peculiar traits
and values, all different today,
and how we once practised
those much simpler things
like manners, now fading away.

I'll think on the traffic,
so thinly spaced,
the crowds of town-goers dressed fine,
and the paper-boy's cry
to all passer's-by;
in that precious childhood of mine.

But, though it's all different
today and now on,
I'm grateful for all that I know,
and cherish the years
as they pass all too swift,
as I think on those days long ago!

Purpose

I found a leaf that had fallen from a tree
Which grew, it seemed, without support,
yet, when looked at more closely -
Grew within a forest of its own;
And each and every tree -
Some old - some new -
Gave strength and shelter to its mate,
Almost lovingly!

I gazed down at that leaf which had begun to die
the moment it was parted from its host;
its single life now ending, but not over,
for it would still have purpose yet,
as, rotting, slowly with others of its kind
New life would spring forth from its nest.
It seemed quite useless there in my hand,
So I laid it gently down to rest.

(I turned, not looking back upon the trees
To find a purpose of my own.)

Sadness is Heavy

Sadness is heavy; it is a pressure on the mind,
A weight on the heart, and an emotion which lingers,
Often, just settling in the cracks of one's being
until it sleeps, soothed by Time's gentle fingers.

Sink Before You Swim!

I found myself in the ocean
As the ship sailed on its way,
And wondered at my action
That found me here, this day.

The water swirled around me
And tried to drag me down;
It had not once occurred to me
That I, this day, might drown.

I only knew I loved you,
But you treated me so cruel;
I believed the lies you told me
Like a weak and virginal fool.

We took the cruise together,
the whole wide world to see.
You couldn't work, so I did,
and paid for you and me.

As soon as we both were aboard
You changed, and I was lost
When I saw you with another girl;
into hell, my love was toss'd.

I stood upon the railing
Looking down into the deep;
My heart was painfully pounding
But just then, I could not weep.

The water looked so empty,
So cold and so forbidding,
Just like your worthless promises,
Oh, who was I really kidding?

I saw you kiss another
And into the sea I fell;
I didn't think that I would jump
From Heaven into Hell.

Now as the ship is leaving
and the water I desperately tread
I wish I'd thought before I jumped
And pushed you in instead!

Slowly, Slowly

Slowly, slowly, through the dream slowly,
I'm softly drifting into the haze
Where today's world melts into fantasy,
And I see the world through that old gaze.

Swiftly, swiftly, the years now go swiftly,
Running, catching, Like wind on a blaze,
Branding my mind with childhood memory,
As my years speed by as if in a daze.

Shortly, shortly, the time will come shortly,
Opening the door of tomorrow's phase
Where Death will present me with a new story,
A new existence with bold, future ways.

Stairway to the Moon

(For Ron 1945-2007)

We saw it,
and, together, we climbed the stairs
all the way to Heaven,
Leaving behind all the fears and phobias
of a lost child's dreams, nightmares
of the waking kind, on our way up out of sight.

We held on fast,
longing to undo the times long gone,
 those years where
All our childhood's tears were left behind,
cured and healthy in our twisted lives,
delivered from that blackest, aching night.

We talked of gentle things,
of memories we'd yet to make as long as fate
Gave us leave to ride that wave without
drowning, in our desperate years,
Which came upon us all too soon.

And there, for one sweet hour,
we grew close, giving the past to the sea
To join the flotsam of that tiring journey
out of sibling rivalry, as we climbed
Together, unforgettably, hand in hand,
the Stairway to the Moon.

Sue

I once heard a story told by an old man
Of 'Why there are stars' in the Sky,
And I find it just fitting when I think of you
So, listen, and I'll tell you why!

There are some special souls of the nurturing kind
Who affect us in different ways
Giving others such joy (with no thought of 'self')
By lighting our darkest of days.

They glow from within, and enjoy what life brings,
If it's 'bad', they turn it to 'good'
They'll listen for hours to us when we're down
And hug us the way a friend should!

There's little they'll ask for themselves day to day,
Except for the right to be free,
And the light that they spread over all those they touch
Will light Heaven for Eternity.

For such light cannot be dimmed, it comes from the soul
And cannot be seen through the day,
So, God, in His wisdom, chose them as his 'Stars'
And each Star, one soul does portray.

So, Sue, take your lantern, as day turns to night,
Cast it out to the Heavens above
To join all the lights from folk such as you
Who light up our night skies with love.

Summer Rain

How pleasant is the summer rain
that taps against my window pane
Delivering me, once again,
From the coldness of alone.

Too often I have sat and cried,
Nurturing my wounded pride
Born of rejection, I must hide
It from the friends I've known.

I gave the best of my life, gladly
To all the ones who've left me, sadly;
How I wish to see them, badly,
Even though they've grown!

That Clever Woman

Where did that clever woman go
Who stood the test of time –
Who managed the impossible alone?
How did she cope with life, back then,
When things often went wrong –
When bank accounts were scraped down to the bone?

Who helped her out, so long ago,
To make ends meet each day –
To find answers to her problems and more?
Well, she's still here and going strong,
Still coping with Life's rule -
But not trying at all to keep the score!

That Old Magpie

'Come up, come up',
I heard the magpie call,
And in my dreams
I struggled to fly up on the wall.

I took a leap but stood quite still,
wishing I could fly
And go up, away from everything,
just like that old magpie!

That Sweet Escape

I will dive into that sweet escape
When it's time to sleep -
And leave behind the nightmare
That is day —
As I drift into the void of night
And the dreams I dare to keep
As I frolic with the Angels
While they play.

I live my best life in those dreams,
As I drift above the clouds
which drape themselves on me,
in Cupid's shape -
To keep me warm and safe from harm
And fill my world with love
From one night to the next
As I make that sweet escape.

That Touch

Oh, that touch –
That wakens those sleeping senses
And electrifies the skin,
Making it reactive and demanding.

That touch –
A new sensation, a foreign event
That causes molecules to collide,
Crash and burn – then re-arrange.

It's too much –
Taking my breath away, giving it back
In snatches that leave me gasping
With emotions – hot and expanding.

It's new –
And leaves me wanting – panting –
Burning for something I never knew –
something I want that is strange.

That connection –
Where two souls meet and gently join
Then rejoin, exploding then imploding
With every breathtaking touch.

The Deck

Not a word was spoken
Nor any remorse felt;
No sign of warm emotion
The winning hand was dealt.
The game was played and won, now,
The dealer had his way,
And raked in all that money -
The takings of the day.

The next hand, it was ready,
The stacked deck set to go
And paid out uniformly
To strike another blow ...
But, like each deception
The loser, too, can win,
For when you choose to forfeit
No one knows what lies within!

The End

I won't die of a broken heart,
For my heart's been often mended.
I will not die alone and sad
As, for years, I was befriended.

I won't die of gross neglect,
Though I suffered my share of strife –
Oh, no, my friends, when I should die –
I'll simply die from life!

The Glory of a Tree

I would sit amongst the trees
On this hot summer's day,
To be where I feel content,
And to keep the heat at bay.

I run my fingers gently
Through the cool earth below
And inhale through my body,
Long and deep and slow.

I take in all the goodness
That's found for miles around,
And let the peace suffuse me
As I sit upon the ground.

The trees play host to many,
Insects, birds and me,
And like the plants that thrive
I am here most willingly.

Man, the curs'd intruder,
Is blind as blind can be,
for he will not appreciate
the glory of a tree.

The Moon and I

I gaze upon a heavenly night
As in the gloom I sit in pensive mood;
the winter moon casts shadows
over mind and soul as I ponder,
And sets my heart alight.

With heavy heart and furrowed brow
I lift my face up in the dark.
We know our place, the moon and I,
No comfort found in each Day's light,
Each of us, alone, somehow.

"When will you show your age, so old,
Moon?" says I, one forlorn night,
"Us Humans start to die at birth -
From Mother's womb to Earth, we go,
Left to rot down in the cold."

The Moon, illuminating all below,
stared down towards the Earth;
There, a voice said soda voce
"You have your friends, and Family, too!
But, I'm alone up here, you know!"

"But, Moon ..." says I with humble voice,
"you have the stars to shine on you!"
"Well, then ..." said Moon "We can't complain,
For each of us has company, though distant,
We should, then, both rejoice!"

The Next Hundred Years

Who knows where we may all be,
one hundred years from now?
Who knows what we'll worship;
the dollar or the cow?
Who knows if there will be a peace
that we've dreamed of for years?
Who knows if smiles will be replaced
by bloodshed and bitter tears?

If this is such a lucky land
of freedom, peace and more,
Then, what the hell is all this talk
of charging off to war?
It seems to me the die is cast,
no matter what we choose,
And, one side may seem to win,
but, really, we'll all lose!

I wonder why we worship Gods,
and behind religion - hide
The truth of how it's meant to be,
so easily pushed aside.
For, peace is simple; peace is cheap,
and I think it's just a joke
That we all play at being 'God'.
We're such pathetic folk!

Ahah! This act, I'm forced to say,
is shallow and absurd,
If behind the scenes the word is 'War!'
(It's such an ugly word!)
Who wrote the script, and made it right
to kill our fellow man,
And blame it on our neighbours,
just because we can?

One hundred years have come and gone
a thousand times before,
Yet, here we are, pathetically,
ripe for another war!
I guess Man's future is in doubt,
so I'll worship the cow,
And pray that it may rule this earth,
one hundred years from now!

The Power of Imagination

When the sky is grey and turning greyer,
Dull in every single way, I take a sheet
Of white sketch paper and draw the sun,
Then, with imagination at work, I bathe
In the sunshine, letting it sink into my skin.

From within, I feel the pretend warmth
Thaw me out, letting me know – without
A doubt – that imagination has a power
To ward off grey skies and become colours
Of the rainbow, preventing showers.

If I believe that the warmth can heal me,
And I feel the healing begin, I can smile
And change the grey to blue, and allow
The precipitation in my heart to pass,
Somehow, overtaken by imagination

The Red Rose

Like blood, the deepest kind of red
That has ever been born or bred,
And whose equal can scarce be found
Even when scattered on the ground.

Whose fragrance lingers in the air
(No other flower can compare).
Protected by the briar and thorn,
The most beautiful of any born?

The Rose; known through history
In verse, and song, and melody -
As a symbol of the lover's heart.
And Love - not easy to impart!

Other flowers of bright array
Mean friendship, given on any day.
But, for true love, none can impose
The message sent by one red rose.

So, lovers all, though rich or poor,
To carry your message to her door -
Don't serenade her, or write prose.
Tell her with just one red rose.

The Sea of Lost Humanity

Fishes and loaves cannot be divided here,
on this cold beach where I lay,
nor will I be saved from the ravaging seas
unless I concede to the lie, and pray.

I have no allegiance to any throne, in truth,
nor am I part of any man's dedicated band,
but, should I fail to succumb to the law,
I'll find myself naked and ruined on the sand.

There is no God in my own heaven
who can help me through any day
as I trudge across life's deserts,
longing to be free just to play.

However, should I forgo the march
and settle on the changeling shore
I might find myself near troubled waters,
wandering forever more.

I long for one good reason to belong
to any worthwhile group or vagrant band,
but I find myself alone, unable to breathe
the salty air that leaves me gasping on the sand.

I am no swimmer, nor can I tread
water or find any purchase at hand
from the restless sea of lost humanity
which leaves me drowning on the land.

The Sloth

He heads for the trees
to find his retreat;
his arms are so long,
but his face is real sweet.

So shy is this creature,
but harmless, I'd say,
and I know that I love
him exactly this way!

In silent retreat
He swings to and fro,
for nothing can harm him
where Sloth's like to go.

We could learn a lesson
How to rid 'us' of wrath
If we took a leaf out of
The life of a Sloth!

The Solitary Storm

A roll of thunder in the night –
A flash of lightning, crisp and bright –
The scent of ozone - a storm coming –
Fat drops of rain on the dry earth – humming.

The threat and danger of a storm –
Light the fire – cosy and warm –
All these things give this season a thrill
And a touch of romance to winter's chill.

But, without company, it's just an event –
Exciting until the drama is spent,
And soon, all things are dry as a bone,
But I'm still here – and all alone!

The Task-Master

I feel thwarted, at times, pipped at the post
Trying to make do with what I have got –
Not grumbling and whinging at what I have not –
Not really sure what I'm after.

I feel tired, frustrated, rarely quite sated
Trying to employ what's within my reach –
And when I can't do – I teach – or preach –
Proving to be quite a task-master.

I'm defeated, and then – retreat into gloom
Trying to cope with all in my power
To spend every waking hour not feeling sour
Contemplating yet another disaster.

I feel strange, for I'm proud of my deeds
As I prove myself capable and worthy
Of making each day count, either by deed
Or by design, and ending in laughter!

The Thief of Time

I lie on the floor, pressing my tiny body
Against the hard frame of the standing clock,
Feeling its rhyme as it keeps perfect pace
With my own brave, fierce little heart.

I run my hand up its smooth surface,
Marvelling at its magnificent body,
Man-made, a work of engineering art,
A puzzle of complex parts, just like me.

My little body thrills to each stroke
As it chimes on the twelfth hour,
My favourite, and I smile and smile,
Still keeping pace with each tick.

In my mind I see inside, listening,
Hearing its Life's force racing away,
never moving from its perfect place
as Grandpa, with his key, opens the door.

One day, I will be old like him and his clock,
But right now, with every tock, I know I am alive
and I rise, touching its face, for we are both blind,
and with a happy heart, I take Time with me.

The Troubled Dream

I slept …
And dreamed a troubled dream
Which found me in a far-off place;
Away, above this life I am,
and haunted by a stranger's face
(Not strange as one I'd never known
But different to the one I knew
And came to love - a one of a kind).
Still haunted yet with dreams of you
I float …
And drift around in time
Still searching for a vital clue -
A key, a door to set me free

So …
Dreaming of a lover new
I wept …
For in this troubled dream
There was no key, nor any door
To set me free.
No life, nor love
Just endless sham -
Entrapped by you forever more.
I slept …
And when I woke - the dream was real.

The Warmth of an Autumn Day

In the warmth of an autumn day
I hear the crows in distant trees;
I hear the wind trying to break in
Through the window, ajar.

Children at play are unaware
Of the warmth of the sun,
Or the birds, or the wind,
Or me, watching from afar.

The wind's howl takes me back
And memories flood my mind,
Filling me with melancholy
And longing for yesterday's sun.

I knew love once, back then,
Though times – hard travelled –
Have brought clarity and truth,
Teaching me that love is hard-won.

I pull a cardigan across my frame
To ward off the chill of old times
And memories and the cold wind,
And close the window at last.

I curl into my good book and chair,
And let memories re-bury themselves
As I embrace the warm Autumn day,
Content to let the past – be past!

The Watchers

The beasts look down from lofty perches
With wicked eyes and taloned haunches,
Waiting to catch evil intruders
And feast upon their souls.

With faces, twisted and distorted,
Intruders know they have been thwarted.
If caught, they will be drawn and quartered!
Such is the gargoyle's goals.

With tethered wings and stony faces
They keep the evil from these places.
Once they strike there'll be no traces,
Except in six-foot holes!

A grimace for a smile, they wait there
And watch for victims, who take no care
Who's keeping guard, this patient pair,
These stoney little trolls!

So, at night, don't ever venture
Out alone, the streets to wander,
Or you might find more than you hoped for;
The guardians of these halls!

The Willow Tree

Winter skies are looming like a bad word of dooming
As I crouch beneath a branch of a despondent willow tree.
As I lean against the cool wood
And whisper that this tree should
pardon my intrusion, and simply comfort me.

Above me it is raining, and the shelter I am gaining
Protects me from the fury of a sudden summer storm,
Whilst I melt into the tree's trunk in clothes,
thank God, all pre-shrunk,
I notice that the tree's skin feels strangely real and warm.

And, later, as I stood there, thankful for the tree's care,
I wondered if I could do a favour in return,
So, when the storm had ended,
to the tree I had befriended,
I promised that, forever, trees would be my real concern.

Many years sped by me, but I often thought of that tree
Standing in the street outside a building of some years,
So, I took a little wander
to that street way over yonder,
And horror turned to dismay, which brought me close to tears.

Where that generous tree had been,
was a signpost, quite obscene,
Standing squat and ugly, where my old friend had once grown.
Stating 'Please protect our trees of all varieties.
Don't deface them or erase them'
signed 'The Mayor of the Town'

I stared at it in wonder, on its message, I did ponder,
And felt a sense of sorrow at how stupid man can be,
Then I saw with hopeful pleasure
that my friend had left a treasure,
For, growing near the sign was a baby Willow Tree!

Through the Crack

I am longer in years than I am in memory,
But in the time of dreams, I drift back
Into another time where fantasy is reality,
And I find myself falling through the mind crack.

To Count The Lucky Starlit Sky

I bend into the gentle breeze
To feel one tender caress
And tip one toe into cool waters
And think of love – more or less.

I lie in the embrace of meadows
And count the lucky starlit sky
As if it held a thousand wishes –
Or even one to get me by.

I climb a mountain of mem'ries
And try to choose the easy road
Where smiles run like those cool waters,
And help lighten that heavy load.

Today's Wonders

How we waste such precious years alone -
wishing, wanting, waiting for another chance
to love, to live, to enjoy.

We sit in darkened and cluttered rooms
filled with trivial things of the past -
longing to relive one old day.

Too many of us cast aside today's wonders
and spend the hours mourning in
discontent, easy to employ.

I would embrace this very minute
should I find myself in good company,
and like a child, lose myself in play.

Traveller of Thoughts

I am a traveller of thoughts,
moving and stretching,
navigating obstacles,
discovering new directions.

I sometimes get lost
or find myself mislaid,
wallowing in a ditch
of unfounded rejections.

But, all is never lost -
or discarded or forgot,
but is carefully considered
through circumspections!

To Turn on a Dime

When things go wrong, how low we often fall,
And doom and gloom colour our worlds
Where storms seem constant, and clouds loom,
Leaving us feeling pallid and wan, above all.

I am knocked off my axis by the slightest thing,
And seem to plummet down into such despair,
And find myself on the verge of depression,
Wondering what the next awful day will bring.

I try not to worry, as worry is a waste of time,
And to look on the brighter side of one's life -
Though most things can be overcome, with help,
I am amazed at how luck can turn on a dime!

Until Mornings' Light

I live for the night
With its wild, wicked ways
Which fades in dawn's fire
Like a sky set ablaze.

I long for the dark
As it crawls o'er the day
and makes itself at home
as if here to stay.

I yearn for the peace
That the dark sometimes brings,
For the truth often hides
In shadows and things.

So, you have the day
And I'll keep the night –
So I can feel safer
Until mornings' light!

Walking With String

I walk the long walk
along a string line
which unravels on my way
as I search for my true home.

It seems, all too well,
I walk alone on this path,
learning who I am -
Accepting what is forecast.

What has gone has ghosts
that linger at my side
from a time long ago,
and lost in dreams.

I hear the screams
of my own self
in those lost days
and cold goodbyes.

But, I have grown strong
along the path
from what was pre-cast -
guided by the string.

So ... I will befriend the dark
and release the string
as I cut myself free
from it and my past.

Warm Summer's Night

I will stir the senses as on a warm summer's night,
and drift across the meadows of your child-like mind,
Leaving behind the first flush of love's embrace,
Like the taste of figs and lavender. Surrender to this night!

Give of yourself all that is free and willing and right,
thrilling to the cold wind that presses against your tepid breast.
Taste the air where the memories of others
Rest as they rise and fall Like the oceans of time.

Feel the rhythm and hear the rhyme of this awakening
Give in to it's unforgiving haste;
do not waste one moment more;
Sit with me and drift away with my caress
As I lift up the curtains of your hesitation.

Do not let procrastination hold you down with false pretences;
Come, rise with me, and I will stir the senses.

Warm Winter's Day

I am warm,
though the air of this young winter's day is cool,
and my face be flushed, though cool to the touch,
And I am worn,
As though over-used, though neglected
As an old pair of slippers
hiding under the bed in the dawn.

I am faded,
though I once was vibrant, coloured primarily
In red, yellow and blue,
though I felt colourless as a book,
One awaiting the word,
also hiding on the bleak, blank page,
Pending the author's imagination –
courage, blame, rage.

I am alone,
though I am surrounded by Life going by,
And I resist the urge to cry,
though tears burn behind eyelids
Which cannot keep out the light,
though the dark hovers by,
Waiting to transform into a warm winter

Where the Passion Lives

Where does the fire come from?
Is it from inside where the passion lives,
Or is it from the heart that yearns
To know the heat of passion, once again,
And to let the mind run free and scream
Out loud, wanting so bad to burn.

Can I quell the fire and let the heart rest?
Or do I continue to daydream, searching
For a love that cannot manifest itself
In the real world where romance fades
And love does not last but drifts away,
And relationships struggle.

If I had a goal, I would strive to gain
Purchase on that slippery slope –
But I have little hope that I could
Reach that goal; but should I succeed
I would say I know best what is good
And what is not, for this struggling soul!

Without Imagination

I write using the theatre of my mind
To find the words ..
Without Imagination, I would not see
The scene
Or hear the players
Or know the plot and outcome …
Without Imagination, there would be
No play!

You Are

You are the warmth when I shiver,
The salve when I burn.
You are the calm in my ocean,
My twist and my turn.

You are the bright in my sunshine,
The moist in my rain.
You are the flight of my freedom,
The smart of my brain.

You are the strength to my weakness,
The kind to my cruel –
You're nobody's mistake,
And never my fool.

You are the tear and the anguish
I cry in my sleep,
You know who you are
And your rivers run deep.

I can't live without you,
But you're not in my debt.
And I always dream of you –
Though we've never met.

I'd call you my shadow
Amongst many things,
For you are the Life
That knowing you brings.

About the Author

I was born in Kalgoorlie, West Australia, in the mid-1900s, the youngest of four children. My family had roots there dating back to the late 1800s, as well as being pioneers in WA. I have travelled a lot around Australia but have never seen Queensland or the Northern Territory, and I doubt I ever will now. But, this adventurous spirit gave me not only a love for history, but a desire to find out where my passion for writing and drawing came from. I still don't know, but it is wonderful to see my children and grandchildren showing an aptitude for art and writing, even the theatre.

Poetry has been an important part of my life, and I have written about many things – those I love, the environment, social issues, even the odd political satire, now and then. It is a wonderful way to express one's feelings and emotions, and my dog, Chushu, a Maltese-x-Schitzu, was my greatest fan until she died. My family were not very encouraging of my work, but many of my friends and those I met along the twisted path of my life gave me the encouragement to improve myself. I have written well over two thousand poems at the last count, but I am pleased to see a great improvement over time, which led me to consider publishing some of them.

My mother made me promise to pursue publishing a book of my favourites (and hers), so – at long last – I have dusted off my old volumes, scanned through the newer ones, and picked out some that seem to suit how I have viewed things over the years.

I am hoping this is just the first of many!

www.ingramcontent.com/pod-product-compliance
Lightning Source LLC
Chambersburg PA
CBHW030328080526
44584CB00012B/760